JESUS THE TEACHER

TOLD BY CARINE MACKENZIE
~ ILLUSTRATED BY JEFF ANDERSON ~

BIBLE ALIVE SERIES: PUBLISHED BY CHRISTIAN FOCUS PUBLICATIONS
GEANIES HOUSE. FEARN. TAIN. ROSS-SHIRE. IV20 1TW. SCOTLAND. U.K.
COPYRIGHT © 2002 CARINE MACKENZIE. REPRINTED 2004.

Jesus taught in lots of places. When he preached everyone was amazed at his knowledge.

He taught out on the hillsides where large
crowds followed him to hear his wisdom.
He even used a fisherman's boat as a
platform to teach the people on the
shore.

Jesus taught wonderful truths about God and heaven and how to live.

The disciples were arguing about who was the greatest in the kingdom of heaven.

Jesus called a little child over. "The one who is as humble as this little child is the greatest in the kingdom of heaven." He said.

When mothers took their children to Jesus, the disciples wanted to turn them away. "Allow the children to come to me," said Jesus, "for the kingdom of heaven belongs to people like them."

Then he took the children up in his arms
and blessed them.

One dark night a leader called
Nicodemus came to ask Jesus some
questions. Jesus told Nicodemus many
wonderful things.

"God loved the world so much that he gave his only Son so that anyone who believes in him shall not perish but have eternal life."

At the well in Samaria Jesus asked a woman for a drink. The woman was surprised. Jesus knew all about her.

"It is not where we worship God that is important," Jesus told her, "but how we worship. We need God's help to worship him as he wants."

Jesus tells us to pray to God who cares for us just like a father cares for his child.

If a child asks his father for a piece of
bread, he will not give him a stone instead.
If he asks for a fish he will not give him a
snake.

Jesus taught us a special prayer we call
the Lord's Prayer.

"Our Father, in heaven
Hallowed be your name.
Your kingdom come.
Your will be done in earth as it is in
heaven.

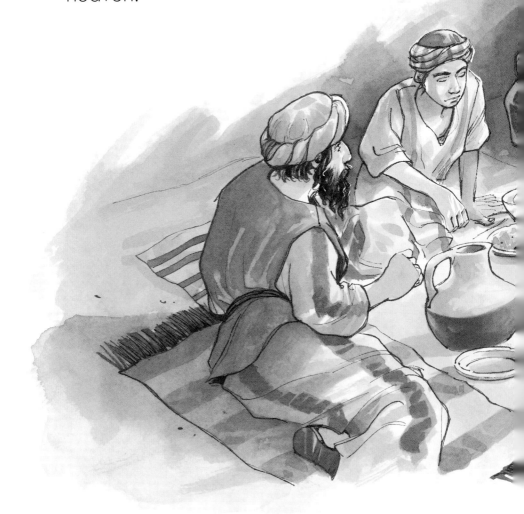

Give us this day our daily bread.
And forgive us our sins as we forgive those
who sin against us.
Lead us not into temptation.
But deliver us from evil."

There is only one way to heaven. Jesus tells us, "I am the way, the truth and the life. No one can get to God the Father except by me."

"I am the door," Jesus said another time. "Those who come in through me will be saved."

"I am the bread of life," said Jesus. "No one coming to me will ever be hungry again, and the person who believes in me will never thirst."

Only Jesus can satisfy the needs and
longings that we have in our souls.

"Which is the most important commandment?"
Jesus was asked one day.
"You must love God with all your heart and
soul and mind and strength." Jesus replied.

"The next one is that you must love other people as much as yourself."

Peter asked Jesus, "How often should I forgive someone who sins against me? Perhaps seven times?"
"No, not just seven times," replied Jesus, "but seventy times seven."

Keep on forgiving those who do wrong to you. Treat other people the way you would like to be treated.

Jesus the wise teacher tells us what to believe. Jesus is the only way to God. Those who believe in him belong to his kingdom. Jesus also tells us how to treat our family and friends. Loving and forgiving is most important.

Matthew 18. Mark 10. John 3.4. Matthew 7.6. John 14.10.6. Mark 12. Matthew 5. Mark 1. Luke 5.